If you were

Alliteration

by Trisha Speed Shaskan

illustrated by Sara Gray

alliteration the same sound repeated at the beginning of two or more words in a phrase or a sentence

PICTURE WINDOW BOOKS
Minneapolis, Minnesota

Editor: Christianne Jones
Designer: Tracy Davies
Page Production: Melissa Kes
Art Director: Nathan Gassman
The illustrations in this book were created with acrylics.

Picture Window Books
5115 Excelsior Boulevard
Suite 232
Minneapolis, MN 55416
877-845-8392
www.picturewindowbooks.com

All books published by Picture Window Books
are manufactured with paper containing at least
10 percent post-consumer waste.

Library of Congress Cataloging-in-Publication Data
Shaskan, Trisha Speed, 1973-
If you were alliteration / by Trisha Speed Shaskan ; illustrated by
Sara Gray.
p. cm. — (Word fun)
Includes index.
ISBN 978-1-4048-4097-3 (library binding)
1. English language—Phonetics—Juvenile literature.
2. English language—Rhyme—Juvenile literature.
3. Alliteration—Juvenile literature. I. Gray, Sara, ill.
II. Title.
PE1135.S53 2007
428.1—dc22   2007044395

Looking for alliteration?

Watch for the big, colorful words in the example sentences.

Special thanks to our content adviser:
Rosemary G. Palmer, Ph.D., Department of Literacy
College of Education, Boise State University

... you could be the "y" sound in a sentence.

A young yak yodels while he yo-yos.

You could be the "z" sound in a sentence.

A zany zebra zigzags across the zither.

If you were alliteration, you would be the same sound repeated at the beginning of two or more words in a phrase or a sentence. You could repeat vowel sounds or consonant sounds.

Ulysses the Unicorn spots a UFO as he makes a U-turn on his unicycle.

6

When Queen Quinn sees the quirky sight, she quits quilting and returns to her quarters.

If you were alliteration, you could be used in common sayings.

pretty as a picture

busy as a bee

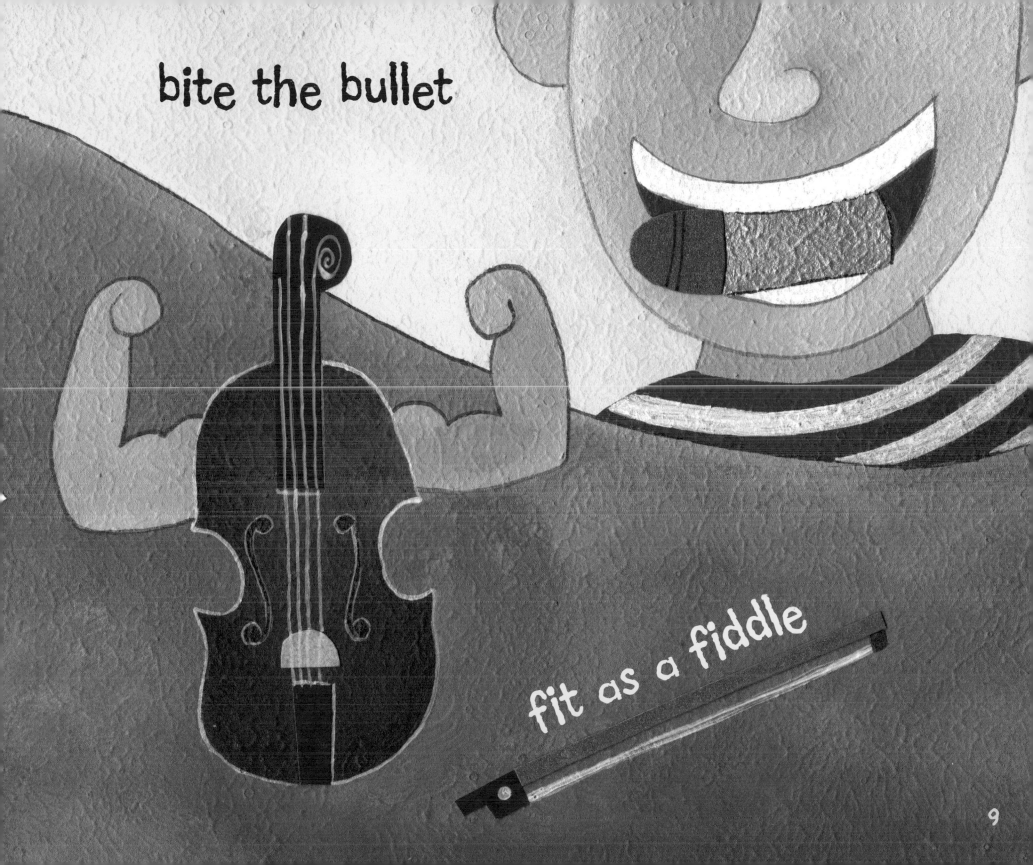

bite the bullet

fit as a fiddle

9

If you were alliteration, you could explore phonics. Phonics shows the relationship between letters and sounds. For example, "ph" can make the "f" sound.

Phillipia the Filly fiddles with the French horn while Frederick takes her photograph.

11

If you were alliteration, you could be two or more consonants that join together to make one sound. For example, you could make the "ch" sound.

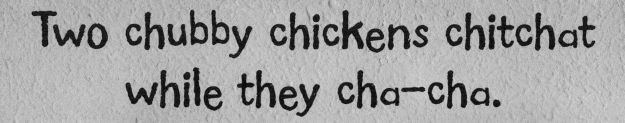

Two chubby chickens chitchat
while they cha-cha.

"Did you see
Chelsea's chicken
house?"

"Cheap."

13

If you were alliteration, you could be two or more consonants that appear together in a word but keep their own sound. For example, you could make the "cr" sound.

Two crazy crows cry at crickets and crocodiles.

If you were alliteration, you could create tongue twisters. A tongue twister is a word, sentence, or phrase that is hard to say because of a series of similar sounds.

She sells seashells by the seashore.

Peter Piper picked a peck of pickled peppers.

The slick snake slithers down the slippery slope.

If you were alliteration, you could be a poem.

A gaggle of geese gather on shore,
graze on the grass,
giggle galore.

19

If you were alliteration, you could tell a story.

Many moons ago lived a mean king named Maxwell. Maxwell demanded macaroni, marshmallows, and macaroons from morning to midnight.

20

He munched and munched
until he became so mammoth
he couldn't move.

You could add a playful punch when you told tremendous tales ...

... if you were alliteration.

Fun with Alliteration

In an acrostic poem, the first letter of each line spells a word vertically. You can make your own acrostic poem using alliteration and your name. On a piece of paper, write your name vertically. Start the first line with your name, just as shown in the example below. Use alliteration in each line by repeating the letter from your name. If you get stuck, look up the letter in the dictionary. The poem doesn't have to be realistic. Perhaps there's an elephant in an elevator, or a turtle driving a truck. Get creative and have fun!

The name "Sam" would look like this in an acrostic poem:

Sam saw a shooting star.
Acrobats like action and adventure.
Many monkeys make money by doing magic.

Glossary

alliteration—the same sound repeated at the beginning of two or more words in a phrase or a sentence

consonants—all letters of the alphabet except vowels

phonics—the relationship between letters and sounds

phrase—a group of words that expresses a thought but is not a complete sentence

tongue twister—a string of words that is difficult to pronounce quickly

vowels—a, e, i, o, u, and sometimes y

To Learn More

More Books to Read
Cleary, Brian P. *Rainbow Soup: Adventures in Poetry.* Minneapolis: Carolrhoda Books, 2004.

Ketteman, Helen. *Armadilly Chili.* Morton Grove, Ill.: Albert Whitman & Co., 2004.

Reynolds, Aaron. *Chicks and Salsa.* New York: Bloomsbury, 2005.

On the Web
FactHound offers a safe, fun way to find Web sites related to topics in this book. All of the sites on FactHound have been researched by our staff.

1. Visit www.facthound.com
2. Type in this special code: 1404840974
3. Click on the FETCH IT button.

Your trusty FactHound will fetch the best sites for you!

Look for all of the books in the Word Fun series:

If You Were a Conjunction
If You Were a Homonym or a Homophone
If You Were a Noun
If You Were a Palindrome
If You Were a Preposition
If You Were a Pronoun
If You Were a Synonym
If You Were a Verb
If You Were Alliteration
If You Were an Adjective
If You Were an Adverb
If You Were an Antonym
If You Were an Interjection
If You Were Onomatopoeia